THE FOOLISHNESS OF ECONOMICS AND THE FINANCIAL MEDIUM OF EXCHANGE.

EARL R. JOSEPH

PREFACE

All things that exist have a foundation of knowledge. This knowledge was not extracted after things came into existence but rather all things was brought into existence from knowledge and all manifestation of knowledge is for a purpose. For all manifested knowledge to fulfill its purpose, its action or course of events must be controlled, influenced or regulated. In other words, it must be governed because the things that were brought into existence are not the source of knowledge but a minute fraction of manifested knowledge.

No manifested knowledge is self-sustaining (I speak here of the universal manifested knowledge) but all manifested knowledge needs a relationship to fulfill its purpose. For instance, the earth needs its relationship with the sun to fulfill its purpose, which is to sustain life. The trees also need a relationship with the earth, sunlight and rain. This is a relationship based on empowerment where one entity is empowering and the other is being empowered. This order of relationship is a simple explanation of the principle that governs the universal manifested knowledge.

It is this principle that sustains the order of the universe.

Man, a minute manifestation of knowledge, has chosen to defy the universal principle of governance and govern himself by the principle of economics and its financial medium of exchange. In his defiance, he has plunged his world into chaos, confusion, pain and suffering.

CONTENTS

The Fascinating Universe

Have you considered the great works that are displayed in the heavens and the depths of the heavens? The miraculous planets and stars that are set suspended in space in their perfect format? How spectacular the order of maintenance is? What principle can maintain such a vast array of solar systems and galaxies with width and depth beyond the imagination of man?

It was once the theory of astronomers that the galaxies with their might of gravity would eventually collide and the universe would end but with the understanding of light and the access of telescopes with which man can observe deeper into space came the discovery of an energy so powerful, that it defied the might of the galaxy's gravity. This energy was shifting the galaxies further away from each other. Scientists in their limited understanding of this energy called it dark energy. They define it as "a hypothetical form of energy that exerts a negative, repulsive pressure, behaving like the opposite of gravity."[1] How remarkable

---

[1] (Swinburne University of Technology, 1999).

is this? What awesome power is this that it defies the might of gravity?

Further to this, in the 1950s and 60s astronomers began to measure the rotation of spiral galaxies. They expected the stars at the galaxy's center to move faster than those at the edge. Yet what they discovered was that the stars at the edge of the galaxy had the same rotational velocity as those near the center. Astronomers believe that another matter beside solid matter is responsible for this effect and they called it dark matter. One of their theories is that

> "[d]ark matter is nonluminous and cannot be seen directly. Thought to make up 27% of matter in the universe, its nature is not well understood. Unlike normal matter, it does not absorb, reflect, or emit light, making it
> difficult to detect."[2]

Astronomers also describe dark matter as

> "...a web-like material interwoven with the regular visible matter. In some places, the dark matter coalesced

---

[2] (University of California - Riverside, 2020)

into lumps. In other places, it stretched out to form long, stringy filaments upon which galaxies appear entangled, like insects caught in spider silk…dark matter could be everywhere, binding the universe together like some sort of invisible connective tissue."[3]

How awesome is this dark matter, with its might of gravitational pull, keeping the stars within the galaxies in harmony, thereby maintaining the perfect order of the galaxies!

Added to this, it is said that the sun is a million times larger than the earth which means that its mass is far greater than earth's and its gravitational pull is very strong. The combination of the sun's powerful gravity and its magnetic force keeps the inner and outer planets in orbit of the sun. How impressive is this mechanism!

Contributing to more than sustaining the planets in orbit, the sun also produces a constant supply of energy. A planet like the earth, which is perfectly positioned within the orbit of the sun, receives the right amount of energy to sustain life.

---

[3] (Harris & Freudenrich, 2007)

The Principle of Order

According to astronomers, the radius from the earth of the observable universe for man is about 46.5 billion light-years away or 4.40×10^{26} m) in any direction [4] with the understanding that the universe is continuously expanding. This revelation teaches us that the universe is larger than we can comprehend and imagine.

What principle then is used to maintain the order and perfection of such a ginormous universe? It is the principle of governance of the universe which displays itself for those who have eyes to see. However, seeing does not always denote understanding.

One of the greatest and most awesome energy witnesses by man is referred to as dark energy. It is through dark matter that the galaxies with their might of gravity and the stars within the galaxies are kept in order. The stars with their tremendous gravitational pull keep the planets in orbit around them and the energy from the stars are beneficial to the planets according to their distance from the sun.

We must understand that a universe with such enormous depth, width, height and

---

4 ("Observable Universe," 2020)

length, which is sustained in order and perfection did not happen by chance but was created. We must also understand that nothing created or made by God is self-sustaining.

Everything that was created or made, was created or made to serve a purpose but cannot serve that purpose as a separate entity. Everything that was created or made needs a relationship to serve its purpose. Take for instance the might of the gravitational pull of the galaxies. It is because of their relationship with dark energy that the galaxies do not collide and end the universe. Consider the stars within the galaxies which are kept in formation because of their relationship with dark matter. Likewise, the planets in the solar system are kept in orbit around the stars because of their relationship with the stars. The earth would not be able to sustain life without its perfect relationship with the sun.

The keyword here is *serve*. Everything that was created or made was created or made to serve a purpose. The principle that governs the universe or the Kingdom of God is the principle that causes all things within the universe to serve or be a servant. This is the principle of righteousness.

To understand righteousness, we must first understand the state of righteous. To understand the state of righteous we must understand exactly what is love.

The Universal Principle of Governance

What exactly is love? I will cut the chase and share it in a more direct manner. We are not speaking here of the love of passion but rather the love of compassion. The love of passion involves your desires and your gain. This has very much to do with self and very little to do with the benefit for others. However, compassion addresses something quite different. What then is compassion? Compassion is "a feeling of deep sympathy and sorrow for another who is stricken by misfortune, accompanied by a strong desire to alleviate the suffering."[5]

The Word of God speaks of the compassion of the Creator, the Almighty God, numerous times. Psalms 86:15 states, "But thou, O Lord, art a God full of compassion". God's compassion is towards men being in the state of prosperity: "Let the LORD be magnified, which hath pleasure in the prosperity of his servant." Psalms 35:27.

---

[5] (The Random House Unabridged Dictionary, 2020)

Love defined is "the state of having compassion towards the prosperity of others". Prosperity here speaks of wholeness, nothing missing, nothing lacking, nothing broken in the spirit nor the flesh. In the case of God, love is "the state of having compassion towards the prosperity of all creation". God knows that without His influence and perfect relationships all things that were created or made will suffer. It is because of God's relationship with His Universal Kingdom that the Kingdom is in perfect order.

What is Righteous?

Being righteous is the pinnacle state of love. It is the state from which the act of love will manifest. Before any action is taken in any situation there must be a judgment. Being righteous is the state of judgment. It is the state where a verdict is decided before the action of love. It is written in the Word of God in John 7:24, "Judge not according to the appearance, but judge righteous judgment." Righteous judgment is always based upon true knowledge, fact and compassion.

True knowledge - knowing that this is God's Kingdom and all things created or made by God must be subjected to the influence of God.

Fact - understanding that most men are not under the influence of God and because of this there is a lot of suffering among men.

Compassion - "a feeling of deep sympathy and sorrow for another who is stricken by misfortune, accompanied by a strong desire to alleviate the suffering."[6]

From this righteous judgment will manifest righteousness or perfect and complete love. Righteousness is the manifestation of love. Righteousness is love that is complete. Righteousness is perfect love because it is complete and pure in goodness. Every time something is given for the prosperity of others, it is the manifestation of love.

All things are received freely and given freely through this manifested love. All things in the Universal Kingdom of God were created to be servants of righteousness. For this reason, "The heavens declare his righteousness" Psalms 97:6.

Servants of righteousness are servants of complete love or servants of selflessness. This principle of righteousness which is also the medium of exchange in the Universal Kingdom of God (all things are given and received by complete love) consistently and continually

---

[6] (The Random House Unabridged Dictionary, 2020)

maintains the order and perfection in the Universal Kingdom of God.

Planet Earth

When compared to the universe, the earth is like a grain of sand and the dominant inhabitant, which is man, is like a microscopic creature.

Let us gaze upon the earth and see which principle man has chosen to govern himself by. With his will to choose and the power to exercise his choice, he has chosen the principle of economics. Economics is a mechanism or an institute of man to attempt to understand his social science concerned with the production, distribution and consumption of goods and services.

The medium of exchange that fuels man's economic principle of governance is the financial medium of exchange called money. How does economics and its medium of exchange work? Man, who has inherited the earth which was not imagined, conceived nor made by him, but by him it was received freely, has chosen to take every good and fruitful thing upon the earth, which was given freely and distribute them through a financial medium of exchange. In other words, man has taken everything which was given to him freely and offered it for sale.

How does this work? Nothing upon the earth was created to be sold but received and given freely by the righteousness of God. The principle of economics and its medium of exchange is a system designed for the gathering of wealth and gaining of power from those who

- hunger
- thirst
- require clothing
- require shelter
- are sick
- are dying

Note that under this system:

- a man cannot eat unless someone profits.
- a man cannot sleep in comfort unless someone profits.
- a man cannot quench his thirst unless someone profits.
- an ailing man can receive no care unless someone profits.

The kingdom of man is governed by the principle of economics and its financial medium of exchange. To survive within this principle, men must become servants of selfish acts, for personal profit, motivated by a desire to succeed or survive.

There is always a victim in the selfish gathering of wealth for personal profit: someone who is exploited, misused or abused. Wealth is gathered from the wants and needs of others. The wants and needs of others are constantly being offered for a price. To pay the price for what is wanted or needed there is a reaction of selfish acts for personal profit in order to purchase what is wanted or needed.

This is the reaction of selfish acts caused by the action of selfish acts. Selfish acts cause reactions of envy, strife, hatred, wickedness, maliciousness, murder, deceit, which ultimately lead to confusion and separation.

Here is the Foolishness of Economics

The earth is filled with the fruits of the righteousness of God, which are the many things created upon the earth for the prosperity of man. There is enough upon the earth that all men can eat and drink, have shelter and clothing and generally live in prosperity and comfort but because of economics and its financial medium of exchange, this is not accessible.

All things manufactured by man are not manufactured for the prosperity of man but the profit of some. To acquire the common things necessary to live in prosperity and comfort under the principle of economics and its financial medium of exchange, there must be a hoarding of the wealth of this world: an accumulation of money, estate, vehicles, houses, buildings and other properties. To hoard the wealth of this world for some is an inadvertent act of selfishness for survival. For others, there is an intentional selfishness and greed within them that cannot be quenched and their accumulation of wealth is never-ending. The effective hoarding of wealth can only be accomplished by acts of selfishness. This is to withhold resources from

- the poor
- the sick
- the widows
- the fatherless
- thy neighbours
- thy friends
- thy brethren

It also means giving only for a price paid in order to secure one's hoard of wealth in a quest for self-aggrandizement. Through this behavior, men have become servants of selfish acts for personal profit motivated by a desire for success or survival.

In this principle, the more things that are made by man, the greater is the demand for the population to acquire these things (a greater financial demand). This means a greater amount of withholding which leads to greater acts of selfishness. For this reason, every generation will be deeper engulfed in selfishness because for every generation there is more to acquire. The governing principle here is that the more things made by man, the greater man's selfishness.

Selfishness breeds ill-will, hatred, anger, despising, vengeance and the like. The effect of economics is poverty, unrest, uprising, protest, corruption, national and international feud, civil wars, piracy, mafia, drug lords, gangsters, warlords, terrorism and wars of nations against nations. As long as the earth is governed by the principle of economics and its financial medium of exchange, it will continue to expand in evil.

The concept of economics and its financial medium of exchange is evil and the application of economics is first ignorance then foolish and less than the foolishness of God: "Because the foolishness of God is wiser than men" 1 Corinthians 1:25.

Forsaking the principle of peace and prosperity, man has gravitated towards the principle of chaos and confusion. For the treasures of this world, men have become corrupt and wicked, in the depth of unrighteousness, lost in their evil ways and hoarders of vain treasures. For the sake of wealth, they have become murders of men, women, children, babies, relatives, family, the sick, the weak, the poor, neighbours, countrymen, citizens. In the foolishness of darkness they have become contractors of evil: deceiving, stealing, destroying; creators of poverty, oppressors. Men have engendered scenarios for pain, anguish, suffering, discord, unrest, hate and vengeance, in their ignorant understanding of governance. They lack discretion, care or compassion and operate in the less than foolish wisdom of the kingdom of ignorance, making decisions in corrupt hearts, towards imperfection, corruption and confusion to the uprisings of conflicts in the dark ignorance of evil for evil, giving birth to evil circumstances.

This is the evil of the kingdom of man; a kingdom built on the full measure of selfishness to facilitate a surplus and distribution of selfishness, rendering men servants of selfishness; a kingdom which has forsaken the truth, governed by the darkness of economics and its financial medium of exchange, manipulated by the capitalists and dictators in communism and socialism.

Let Us Imagine for a Moment

Imagine a few residential buildings amid a massive estate and all who reside there are relatives. Some of them are builders, tailors, maintenance workers, some are cooks, others are cleaners, animal farmers, crop farmers and some are laundry workers. Imagine the crop farmers farming for all who reside on the estate; the animal farmers farming for all who reside on the estate. The point is to imagine all the workers on the estate labouring for the benefit of all who reside on the estate. This means that none on the estate will be without a house, none will be without food and other necessities. This simply means that none on this estate will be lacking the things that are necessary to live in comfort.

Think of a village in this scenario, a town or even a city. The truth is, in ancient times there were tribes who lived like this and these tribes were considered as uncivilized. What should we say about this present day, with man's governance of economics where so many people are homeless, so many are refugees, so many are starving, so many are being evicted daily? There are millions of people who are in dire circumstances because of economics and its financial medium of exchange.

This governing system is like a trojan horse designed by the enemy of man to infiltrate the heart of every man causing men to function by selfishness and some with greed and others a great measure of greed that cannot be quenched. This is a system designed to cause separation and confusion even among families, relatives and friends, in communities, in towns, cities, countries and even among countries. This trojan horse has infiltrated the world and is rapidly bringing out the worst from within men.

The enemy of man has little to do but look and rejoice as men destroy themselves. This is a display of man's ultimate battle between good and evil and in the kingdom of man evil is the champion.

How Divided We Are

Economics and its financial medium of exchange has destroyed the relationships of men. This has caused the failure of the strong to empower the weak. It has placed us in socioeconomic divisional brackets as poor, middleclass, upper-class, millionaires and billionaires. With every generation it has navigated men to a decrease in civility, having less compassion, less kindness, becoming unfriendly and indifferent, despising good and embracing what is ungodly. Our so-called civilized society is being populated with uncivilized men.

The truth is the microscopic dominant inhabitant of the earth man, in his pico fraction of the universal kingdom, has chosen to defy the principle that governs this ginormous universal kingdom. Can a grain of sand on the shoreline defy the rising tide? Surely, it cannot.

Excuse me if I said that economics and its financial medium of exchange is foolishness. I was wrong. It is less than foolishness! Even those who think they have great power in the earth, who live in a bubble of enormous wealth, without a care of the crumbling society around them, the same crumbling society that sustains their bubble, would be dumbfounded in the realization that they cannot escape when the uncivilized civil society is utterly consumed by evil.

For leaning on their knowledge and understanding and forsaking the knowledge and understanding of God the Creator, men would perish because in the knowledge and understanding of men there is much ignorance. The evidence that men are incapable of governing themselves without the relationship of God their Creator cannot be disputed. The intentions and methods of man's governance are wicked and full of evil. Within the application of economics and its financial medium of exchange there is no righteousness nor joy and at its end, there is no peace.

Know this, in the currency of the Kingdom of God, which is righteousness or complete love, there is no recession, no inflation nor deflation. The effect of righteousness is joy, perfection and peace.

The power of choice has been given to all men, but to whom do you choose to pledge your alliance, the kingdom of man, which shall perish or the Kingdom of God, which shall prevail?

References

Harris, W. & Freudenrich, C. Ph.D. (2007, September 4). *How Dark Matter Works.* HowStuffWorks.
https://science.howstuffworks.com/dictionary/astronomy-terms/darkmatter.htm

Observable Universe. (2020, December 12). In *Wikipedia.*
https://en.wikipedia.org/wiki/Observ

able_universe

Swinburne University of Technology. (1999).
    Dark Energy. In *Cosmos – The SAO
    Encyclopedia of Astronomy.*
    https://astronomy.swin.edu.au/cosmo
    s/D/Dark+Energy

The Random House Unabridged Dictionary.
    (2020). Compassion. In *dictionary.com.*
    https://www.dictionary.com/browse/
    compassion?s=t

University of California – Riverside. (2020,
    September 9). *Physicists explain
    mysterious dark matter deficiency in galaxy
    pair: Self-interacting dark matter theory
    explains why two galaxies have less dark
    matter than others.* ScienceDaily.
    www.sciencedaily.com/releases/2020/
    09/200909132101.htm